TAKE MY MONEY, PLEASE

MY 21-DAY GIVING PROJECT

ARUNA GOBALAN

COZY LAVENDER PRESS

Copyright © 2020 by Aruna Gobalan

All rights reserved.

No part of this book may be reproduced in any form or by any electronic or mechanical means, including information storage and retrieval systems, without written permission from the author, except for the use of brief quotations in a book review.

To those who doubt themselves.

I turned out okay (I think). You will too.

CONTENTS

Introduction — vii

1. Day 1: Happiness — 1
   Aunt May
2. Day 2: Music — 4
   Is There Anything You Cannot Learn Online?
3. Day 3: Reading — 8
   The Internet Before the Internet
4. Day 4: Black Thumb — 12
   How Many Cacti Have I Killed So Far?
5. Days 5 and 6: Groceries — 16
   Searching the Refrigerator for the Answer to Life's Problems
6. Day 7: Educators — 20
   Those Who Willingly Choose to Be Interrupted Every Ten Seconds
7. Day 8: Trash — 24
   When the Garbage Goes Out More Than You Do
8. Day 9: Plan C — 28
   Sometimes Opportunity Comes Knocking. Literally.
9. Day 10: Packages — 32
   Making Santa Look Like a Slacker
10. Day 11: Sanity — 36
    The Secret to a Happy Marriage: A House-Cleaning Service
11. Day 12: Saints — 40
    If You Cannot Feed a Hundred People, Feed Just One
12. Day 13: Inner Peace — 43
    It's Not What You Think
13. Day 14: Firefighters — 47
    What the Bravest Go On to Become
14. Day 15: Perspective — 51
    If You Can't Pay It Back, Pay It Forward
15. Day 16: Theory Of Motivation — 55
    Maslow and the Ovarian Lottery
16. Day 17: Self-Care — 60
    How to Build Self-Confidence: Get Your Hair Done

17. Day 18: Clash of Cultures *Caught Between Two Worlds*	64
18. Day 19: Dining Out *Yes, I Sometimes Fast. Between Meals*	70
19. Day 20: Medical Diaries *Why I Tried to Adopt a Nurse*	74
20. Day 21: The Very End *The Not-So-Grim Reaper*	79
Afterword	81
Notes	85
Acknowledgments	87
About the Author	89

INTRODUCTION

I woke up on a crisp fall morning with a case of the *blah*s. Life felt like an endless ocean of beige. There have been times in my life when I've longed for this kind of stability and routine. Not this Sunday, though. I felt shackled by monotony.

In the middle of a raging global pandemic that has wreaked havoc on people's lives and livelihoods, I wasn't alone in feeling trapped. But it felt like it.

Reluctantly, I stared at my to-do list. The list said I needed to meditate. Stat. One thing I've learned over the years is to not argue with my to-do list. My list has invisible tentacles that poke and prod me, rather unpleasantly, when I don't listen.

So, I set my timer to twenty-one minutes and sat down to meditate. Why twenty-one? A minute to fidget, twenty to meditate. I call this wishful planning. If only we could live our lives with such precision!

After fidgeting for seven to eight minutes, I finally settled. Somewhat. And then it hit me. A giant wave of emotions—

INTRODUCTION

guilt for being healthy and financially sound during a difficult time for so many and an undercurrent of anxiety about what lay ahead, worried that it was just a matter of time before this good fortune of ours would change. But then, unexpectedly, I felt a jolt of inspiration. I had an idea for how I could *do* something to make a difference. And finally, I felt joy, selfish as it sounds, to be relieved from the dreaded monotony I woke up to.

I willed myself to sit through the remainder of my meditation session, excited to put my plan into action. This is, of course, precisely the opposite of what you're told to do in meditation. I was reflecting on the past and planning my future instead of staying present. Oh, well. At least I had a path out of *beigedom*, out of the *blah*s.

When my meditation timer went off, I sprang up to nurture the seed that had just been sown.

The *Giving Project* was born.

∽

The universe has many selfless people—people who drop everything and go out of their way to help others in need. I know some of them. Unfortunately, I'm not one of them. I prefer to stay in my bubble and let everyone handle their own problems.

Through the Giving Project, I hoped to make small financial gifts for twenty-one days to acknowledge the contributions of various unsung heroes around me while also personally thanking them.

Sometimes, there's a lot of drama, like tears and such, when you recognize someone's contribution. I'm anti-drama. I like avoiding tears, even happy ones. Also, generosity typically causes people to reciprocate with compliments, and I don't particularly take to those well, either. Sometimes I know the compliments are not genuine, and at other times my impostor syndrome gets the better of me.

So, this project was born to confront, dare I say it, my selfishness, and to bring myself out of my comfort zone, even if just a teeny bit.

Though I was hoping it wouldn't, the COVID-19 pandemic influenced the project significantly. The pandemic was the attention-seeking elephant in the room that I could not avoid. Let's just say I worked with (and around) it as much as possible.

Every project needs a scope. Here are some parameters and ground rules I established for this exercise:

- While giving can take many forms, I decided to start with **financial giving**. Gift-giving in the form of money is a safe option. The value is objective and usually makes recipients happy, albeit briefly.

- The project would be **twenty-one days** long. Twenty-one days is a Goldilocks number—not too long, not too short.

- I chose to give between **fifty and one hundred dollars** each day. That's not a trivial amount of money over twenty-one days. And especially for me, because I love a deal. I spend more time figuring out the best price on a toaster than toasting. So, parting

INTRODUCTION

me from my money isn't easy. Fifty to a hundred dollars leaving my wallet every day ensured I invested myself emotionally in this project.

- Where possible, I'd **give in cash** to learn both the pleasure the recipients get with receiving money and see if there's any pain when the money leaves my wallet every day.

- As much as possible, I'd direct the giving to **one person** each day. I figured this would be more impactful than spreading the money among a few people.

- In addition to the money, I'd try to **personally thank** the recipient, to let them know they are appreciated. This, I knew, would test my comfort-zone.

- I'd keep the project a secret until completion. I didn't want to be influenced by anyone, not even family. So, I decided **not to tell anyone** else about this project until the end.

- I'd take time to **pick recipients** to ensure unsung heroes in my life are recognized.

- With brutal honesty, I'd **record** each gift to examine how it impacted the recipient and me.

INTRODUCTION

WHAT THIS BOOK CONTAINS

In this book, you'll find twenty essays—one for each day of giving (and one for two days: there's one essay that combines two related subjects).

What started initially as simple observations about the Giving Project took a turn into personal (sometimes deeply so) recollections and annotations on various topics. Research has shown that being empathetic triggers memory recollections since empathy and autobiographical memory share common neural pathways.

I learned a lot about myself through this process; the experience was immensely cathartic. I did not realize, for example, that I had so many childhood memories until I started reflecting on what some of these giving experiences meant to me. In that sense, this is a quasi-memoir.

A few of these musings are silly, some are shallow, some are comical, a few are deep, but all are honest. This book is like an Indian *masala* film—a little bit of everything—agony, humor, joy, misery, anxiety. Not by design, but I guess that's what life is: a cocktail of emotions.

The people in this book are real, but I've changed names or generalized some observations to shield their privacy. I've tried hard to keep the authenticity of the experience intact, though.

You don't have to read these essays in sequence, nor do they all have to be read in one sitting. So, feel free to dip in, dip out, and jump to a story that catches your eye.

My hope is you'll enjoy reading this as much as I enjoyed writing it. If nothing else, I hope I can make you laugh for a bit. If not with me, at me. I'm okay with that.

INTRODUCTION

Hopefully, I can also inspire you to undertake similar giving projects of your own.

The world has too many takers. It is in desperate need of more givers.

DAY 1: HAPPINESS

AUNT MAY

I cannot say enough good things about my local outdoor farmer's market, especially in the summer. As a lifelong vegetarian, I delight in fresh, local produce. That it's cheap, too, is just icing on the cake.

When the pandemic hit, one of the first things to shut down in my community was this market. It gutted me. I whined about it to just about everyone I knew. People were distraught at bars shutting down; I lamented the lack of kale —of course, a very Californian thing to do.

Amidst the sea of vendors at the market, one in particular is my favorite: an older Asian lady who doesn't speak much English. While other vendors pleasantly try to sell you their produce and answer your questions, she has the bedside manner of an army general dealing with insubordinates. If you hover around her stand, she'll yell you into submission (and convince you to buy some carrots).

But you can tell she has a heart of gold. And the kindest eyes. I missed her during the shutdown. I worried about how she'd cope without the income from the market.

Eventually, the market reopened with a ton of new rules and precautions. Masks were required and stalls were double-spaced. I was thrilled to be back, of course. My joy was tempered, though, with concern for the vendors out there risking an infection. They were selling produce because their livelihood depended on it. That made me feel even guiltier.

So, it was a no-brainer that I chose Sergeant Broccoli Lady to be the first recipient in the Giving Project. I don't know her name. I'm too chicken to ask. So, I'll just call her Aunty May. That has a nice ring to it.

Cash in hand, I went to the market with my husband. I sent him off in another direction while I hung around Aunty May's stand to see if she'd have a lull in customers. She didn't. She was in peak form, bellowing prices out to anyone who dared to ask. Finally, I worked up the nerve to approach her.

What happened next is embarrassing, to put it mildly. I stuffed the money into Aunty May's hands. She looked at me, quizzically. We both had face masks on, so she couldn't quite see me fully. Thank goodness! I mumbled, somewhat incoherently, about it being a gift to say "thank you." I told her I was doing a giving project. Like that would make any sense to anyone! Cripes! She started to look a little alarmed. So, I did what anyone with common sense would do in that situation. I bolted.

Instead of making an older woman happy, I likely scared the wits out of her. I'm pretty sure she thought I was returning some cash that had fallen off her cash box. Or that I was a weirdo. Oh well. I deserved it.

I hope she kept the money.

THIS EPISODE CONFIRMED that I find giving almost as uncomfortable, if not more uncomfortable, than taking. Some people give gracefully. I'm the definition of awkwardness in giving.

The interchange with Aunt May was awkward, maybe even funny, in retrospect. It confirmed the unease I feel in emotionally charged social situations.

I'll just let my husband make trips to the market in the foreseeable future, or at least until Aunt May can completely forget the incident. She probably has already.

In the meantime, I was glad to have checked off day one.

DAY 2: MUSIC

IS THERE ANYTHING YOU CANNOT LEARN ONLINE?

*G*rowing up, for over fifteen years, I took music lessons to play the veena, an Indian string instrument.[1]

Took is about as neutral a word as I can think of to describe the experience. I wasn't given a choice in the matter; that's how things were back then in my family. I did not know I could complain or whine my way out, either (my daughter taught me that lesson decades later).

As it happens, if you spend fifteen years doing something, you're bound to become reasonably decent at it. Considering I was then a young child (and children have sponge-like learning abilities), I *used to* be quite adept at playing the veena.

Then, life happened. I moved across many cities, then various countries, and eventually multiple continents. Somewhere along the way, my vintage veena joined me. For more than a decade, it's been with me, serving as a decorative item and a conversation piece for when guests visit. They invariably ask who plays it. I always say, "I used to,"' and then deflect the conversation to hot soup or other such worldly matters.

It wasn't that I didn't try to play. I did. I pulled up my notes from the last century and tried. My fingers moved like they had arthritis on a cold, winter day. I couldn't read the music notes.

I'd heard analogies about how once you learned to read or play music, it was like riding a bike and your brain would know what to do when you returned to it. Rubbish.

There was a silver lining, though. In the years I was slowly losing my musical abilities, I had made some progress on my athletic ones. I never missed a chance to proselytize about the power of exercise to all who cared to listen. Around this time, I also read several articles and books on music's ability to invigorate brain cells, especially middle-aged ones.

So, I decided to swallow my pride and re-learn the veena as a beginner instead of an expert. My original teacher had died a few years ago. No one else would feel sorry for me starting over. Honestly, no one else would care.

I knew I didn't have the time in my schedule to attend classes in person. So, I looked up online options. I felt like Rip Van Winkle, waking up after twenty years in hibernation. *I discovered online YouTube video tutorials.* There were So. Many. Choices. Why hadn't I known this all along? Never mind, don't answer that.

I picked a few super-short beginner pieces and started to learn at my own pace. Translation: V E R Y S L O W L Y. What used to take me a couple of hours to learn as a twelve-year-old now took me two days. But I was in no hurry. I persisted. Slowly but surely, with practice, my fingers started to find their way across the frets.

Miraculously, I got better. When I play a piece now, it resembles music instead of a bunch of disjointed sounds. Now, I'm grateful to my parents for having forced me through those lessons all those years. Hindsight, as they say, is 20/20.

I've gotten confident enough to post some of my music clips to my social media feeds. Go figure.

For my second day of giving, I decided to write a personal thank-you note with a small donation to an owner of one of the music websites I use consistently. She has a staggering amount of good content on her online channel: tutorials, lessons on music theory—the works. And incredibly, she doesn't charge for any of this.

I felt sorry for her, too. Instead of simply saying thanks, people fill her videos' comments with requests (demands) for more tutorials. Talk about "looking a gift horse in the mouth." I guess I was keen to separate from this crowd.

I found her number online and reached out to her via text message. I explained how I had completely lost touch with music, and how her videos and tutorials helped me get back on track. I let her know how gifted she was (because she truly is) and that her work is much appreciated.

Then, I asked her for her account details to send her some money. I'm guessing at this point, she balked. I probably sounded like a Nigerian prince promising a kingdom in return for bank account details. To reassure her I was genuine, I told her I wasn't an internet scammer. A lot of detail about me not being a Nigerian princess or, for that matter, any princess. I'm guessing the word *cuckoo* crossed her mind.

Either out of pity or to stop me from rambling, she obliged. She sent me her account details. I wired some funds over to her. I told her it was a form of *guru-dakshina* (*guru*—teacher; *dakshina*—a gift or a donation), an Indian tradition to honor your teacher at the completion of your learning. Never mind that my education had just (re)started.

Then, I spent the day overthinking my giving. Did I set high expectations and then let her down by not sending enough money? Since I had made such a big deal about giving, should I not have given more? Did I offend her?

I'll never know because that was the extent of my conversation with her. I intend to remain a faceless subscriber.

Obscurity is my comfort zone.

DAY 3: READING

THE INTERNET BEFORE THE INTERNET

I love to read. I also love free stuff. So, it's not a surprise that the local library is my definition of paradise on earth.

Books have always fascinated me. Two people (both no longer with us) in my life are primarily responsible for fostering my love of reading—my dad and my English teacher. They encouraged me to read different genres, even as a child. Resources were limited, but they made sure I was never short of reading material.

Times were simpler, too. The numerous digital distractions that compete with kids' attention for reading these days didn't exist back then. The only options we had were—read, go outside and play, or be bored.

A vivid memory from those days was how my childhood best friend, who also happened to be my neighbor, and I, decided to form our own "library" when we were ten since we didn't have access to one close to our homes.

TAKE MY MONEY, PLEASE

One summer, we gathered up all the books we could find. Anything that resembled a book became a candidate. Our own and our parents' books were the first to be consigned to our library. Then, we went door to door around the neighborhood and asked neighbors to donate books—kind of like nerd Halloween, trick-or-treating for books instead of candy.

Having gathered up around two hundred books, we went about inscribing the words "Bharat Circulating Library" inside the cover of every book. The country (India) was referred to as Bharat (and still is, locally) before foreign invaders conferred the name "India". That's right—we weren't building a teeny, weeny local library. We were building a national one.

With those words etched in ink, the books became the property of the library. We dusted off some shelves in my friend's house and set up our library. We made plans to charge a (nominal) fee for membership and even developed a notebook-based checkout register. People could come in and check out books they liked, but had to return them by the due dates. Our proposed fines for late returns were insanely high; I don't remember the number exactly, but it was multiple times the membership cost. I guess we were scared of losing all the books we'd collected.

It was either the threat of fines (the no carrots, all sticks approach) or flawed marketing, but I don't really remember the registers filling up ever. Or, for that matter, anyone checking out a single book. Or, it could have been that school started back up, relegating the library to the back of our would-have-been patrons' minds.

Eventually, the library dissolved on its own, and some of my dad's books made it back to his bookshelf, albeit still displaying "Bharat Circulating Library" proudly on the cover page.

∽

GIVEN this longstanding love for libraries (my own included), it's no wonder I wanted to incorporate some library-related giving as part of this project. In my opinion, national parks and libraries are the most under-appreciated resources in our country.

With an ever-growing amount of digital content that you can directly download to devices, you're right to wonder about the value of a physical library building anymore. Gone are the days, though, when the library was simply a place for you to read quietly or a place to get books to read quietly at home. Equating the library to a collection of books these days is akin to saying the iPhone is a device used to make phone calls. That too, but much more.

Libraries have become centerpieces for communities, offering books, yes, but also free internet, classes, events and more, especially to the underprivileged and underserved members of our society. I'm not sure about the doctor's office, but the library has a cure for every malady. You just have to know where to look.

Since I was keen on giving to people, where possible, rather than institutions, I decided to head over to my local library to find a way to tip a librarian. With the pandemic, libraries have had to rethink their physical book lending policies to ensure compliance with public health guidelines. Patrons now schedule book pickups, and a library worker brings the books out to an outside table at the assigned time—as if they didn't have enough to do already!

When a worker at the library—someone who I'd never seen before—brought my material to the table, I told her I was keen on donating. She asked me if I wanted to contribute to the library. I said, "No. I want to make a personal donation, to someone, anyone." Then I added, "As a thank you, because times are tough." Naturally, she seemed confused.

Then I asked if she could take my donation. She seemed taken aback but finally said thanks and accepted the money. I managed to mumble a "No, thank YOU" before scampering away.

I could definitely have been less awkward. But you can't change a lifetime of ingrained habits overnight. I didn't have access to the people I usually see at the library, so I clumsily gave money to this unknown worker. At least I didn't have to worry about what the librarian I usually encounter would think of me.

However, since I can never worry too much, I wondered if I should have given the money to someone more deserving. What if I had just tipped a sub who happened to be at the only library shift of her entire life?

A *Gita* (Indian spiritual text) verse comes to mind:

> *Karmanye Vadhikaraste,*
>
> *Ma phaleshou kada chana*

Translation: Your rights are to actions only, not to the fruits (or consequences) of your efforts.

In other words, do what you're supposed to do and move on.

DAY 4: BLACK THUMB

HOW MANY CACTI HAVE I KILLED SO FAR?

As a lifelong vegetarian, you'd think I'd have great chemistry with plants. It turns out, my relationship with Kingdom Plantae is more parasitic than symbiotic. On the color gradient, my thumbs are closer to the black end of the spectrum than the green end. Sadly, I'm married to someone with similar traits.

I grew up as an urban kid. Though we weren't far away from farmlands and rich soil, the house I grew up in didn't have a green patch. That said, we had a ton of potted plants lining the perimeter of the house. Thankfully, they did not depend on me for sustenance. Suffice to say I didn't learn much about gardening in my youth.

Later, my husband and I had jobs that took us around the world and many rental apartments ensued. Eventually, when we went house hunting for our starter home, I laid out exacting preferences, a mile-long-checklist of *features* I wanted in the home. Not surprisingly, "low-maintenance yard" topped that list, leading our realtor to remark that we were DINKS (a '90s acronym for "double income no kids") looking to drown in wine on Fridays and travel often. Not quite. He just didn't understand my fear of growing plants. But he found us the home we wanted. Close to, but not in the city.

Our new home backed up to a forest reserve—a win-win situation. We had all the greenery we wanted with no maintenance required from us. What's not to love about that? We settled in and enjoyed the house and our very private nature-maintained reserve. But soon, as luck would have it, we had to move across the world for our jobs again.

Our next home, a larger American-size single-family home, did come with a yard and a lawn. And a homeowner's association with military-level maintenance standards. Not long after we moved in, I found myself Googling things like *Can you revive dead grass?* or *How to kill weeds easily?* The mint I lovingly planted in my herb garden went wild and threatened to take over the entire block.

Desperate, we turned to our neighbors to ask for recommendations for a gardener. That's how we found Juan. He's taken care of our yard and lawn for close to fifteen years now. Juan helped plant a few baby plants in the yard; they are mature trees now. He didn't have kids back then; now, he has four.

We also saw his business grow. Juan started off doing all the work by himself, but now he has a three-man crew with him. Sometimes months would go by before I'd have any conversations with Juan other than writing him a check. At other times, Juan and his men would be in and out of the yard before I had time to register the sound of the lawnmower.

Every so often, I'd notice an unkempt yard just a day or two before hosting a backyard party and would desperately call Juan to see if he could come by.

Those phone conversations usually went something like this: Juan asks me which house I'm referring to. He has never had much reason to learn my name—just my yard and its quirks.

Juan takes care of many other homes in the neighborhood. All homes look similar. I think one of the Homeowners Association's unpublished rules is "You may paint your house any color you like, as long as it looks exactly like your neighbors.'"

So, when Juan asks me which house I was referring to, he means, "What trees are in the backyard?"

I tell him the truth: I don't know the names of the trees in the yard since he was the one who planted them. Stalemate.

So, we try again. A game of context clues ensues. Years ago, I had asked Juan for a fruit tree to be planted in the yard. He planted a plum tree. In all these years, I still haven't seen a single plum from that tree. So much so I've forgotten it's a *plum* tree. So, when he asked me if it was the house with the *plum* tree in the center, it took me a while to realize that he was indeed referring to my house. Anyway, the mystery was solved—he finally knew who he was talking to.

Juan then wants to know when I need the yard tidied up. My answer to this question usually varies between "today" and "tomorrow." Silence. I wait with bated breath.

To date, Juan has never said, "Poor planning on your part does not constitute an emergency on my part," at least, not to my face. I'm sure he must have thought it, though. I would have if I were him.

He soon turns up with his crew, and they're at it for a while. My backyard gets an instant makeover. It's like the before and after pictures in a home improvement magazine. I'm always grateful. He has never let me down.

So, when I heard the lawnmower this time, I headed outside casually, like I was going to get the mail. Juan was taking care of the neighbor's driveway. Without much hesitation, I walked up to him and handed him some money. He looked up, quizzically. I managed to blurt out that times were tough, and it was just a tiny token of appreciation. He took it. Said he was thankful.

He then went on to talk about his family. Four kids. He admitted it was tough. Especially with the pandemic, several people had canceled their services. He had to pay his employees. I nodded. I felt his pain. Even though we had masks on, his eyes told the story. Something stirred deep in me. Gratitude. For a lot of things. He said he'd take care of the weeds soon. I knew that wasn't the point.

I was happy to have had the courage to do this face-to-face, albeit half-masked. I didn't care whether Juan took care of the weeds or not. It didn't matter to me then. I'd worry about the weeds next time there was going to be a backyard party.

I waved him away and headed back.

Juan still doesn't know my name. Don't think he ever will. And that's cool!

DAYS 5 AND 6: GROCERIES

SEARCHING THE REFRIGERATOR FOR THE
ANSWER TO LIFE'S PROBLEMS

When the pandemic hit, like many others, my family and I stayed indoors. Something as innocuous as a trip to the grocery store now required a spacesuit. But, avoiding the store wasn't an option since, ironically, when the front door is shut, the pantry and refrigerator doors are opened, instead, with alarming frequency. This required a revamp of our food stock replenishment strategies since, prior to the pandemic, we made far fewer trips to the grocery stores.

To avoid store trips, I turned, like the rest of the world, to grocery delivery apps. But there were a few hiccups with outsourcing my grocery shopping.

My shopping lists tend to be non-standard because of some self-imposed rules. These are aspirational, of course. I wish I could follow them all the time. That said, these five rules may be the only diet and nutrition advice you'll ever need in life *if* you can be steadfast about shopping under these constraints.

- "If it's in your house, it's in your mouth." The best

way to avoid junk food is not to bring any into your house in the first place.

- Shopping for groceries when hungry is a good way to end up bringing home the entirety of Aisle 7.

- Make a list before you shop so you don't buy stuff like you're an unsupervised five-year-old with a one-hundred-dollar bill.

- Stick to the perimeter of the store; that's where the healthier stuff is. The middle aisles are for increasing your middle.

- Limit the number of shopping trips to the store to resist temptation by consolidating purchases

Like most things in life, the simplest-sounding advice is often the hardest to adhere to.

The above rules, especially the one about shopping the grocery store's periphery, make it difficult to order online. But I tried using delivery apps.

My food-delivery shopping experiences usually went something like this: I'd place an order in the online app, and before long, my *shopper* would be at the store. Then, through no fault of hers, she'd have trouble finding eighty-five percent of the items on my list. Frantic chats would ensue between us; product swaps suggested and rejected—the equivalent of ordering from the menu at a restaurant and then badgering the waiter with a ton of substitutions.

I'm sure some shoppers signed up for fifteen-minute gigs and ended up, annoyingly, spending a whole hour on my list.

After a couple of such shopping mishaps, I had a choice. Either standardize my grocery lists to make it easier for others to shop my list or go to the store myself. I chose the latter. Armed with masks, gloves, sanitizers, and wipes, I ventured out to the stores.

I felt pretty proud of myself, like I was going above and beyond to answer my call of duty to the family. Until, that is, I walked into the store and saw the store employees.

These grocery store workers provide new meaning to the phrase *in the eye of the storm.* They don't have the option to *Instacart* (or equivalent grocery delivery services) their jobs away. Odds are a good number of these employees have high-risk people in their families, yet they show up at work day in and day out, risking their lives to stock store shelves so we can go crazy and hoard toilet paper.

I knew right at the beginning of this project that grocery store workers belonged on my list. Once I was at the store, though, I became nervous about handing over money to a random person.

I wanted to avoid a scene by giving in front of an audience. So, I roamed the aisles quite a bit. Eventually, I found a worker stocking milk in the refrigeration section. It was quiet around him. I walked up to him, handed him the money, and told him I appreciated his doing this difficult and now outright-dangerous job. He said he couldn't take the money. I insisted. I told him it would make *me* feel better if he did. Eventually, very reluctantly, he did and thanked me. I quickly exited the store to avoid being spotted!

Mission accomplished. I had forgotten to get milk in the process, but there was always going to be another trip. Buoyed by the success here, I wanted to keep going because I felt that one donation wasn't enough. Grocery store workers are so central to our existence that I felt I owed at least two of the twenty-one days of this project to honor store workers.

MY NEXT STOP was to tip the unsung hero—the grocery store cart pusher. Not only do they retrieve carts from far-flung corners of the lot, but with the pandemic, they also had the additional job of disinfecting the carts each time.

Bravely, I ventured to the parking lot at Costco. If there's one thing about Costco parking lots, it's that they are full. All. The. Time. Again, avoiding the crowds, I located a cart pusher in a relatively quiet corner of the lot. I told him I was grateful for his service and hoped he'd accept my small thank you gesture. He was surprised but took it with a smile.

I headed back home, feeling relieved and hoping I had generated a little goodwill all around.

There are so many unsung heroes right in our midst. We need to wake ourselves up from our bubbles and acknowledge their existence. It doesn't take much to bring someone else joy, even if it's just for a brief moment.

I FELT a lot of joy in giving. I also realized that giving invokes far greater pleasure than receiving.

DAY 7: EDUCATORS

THOSE WHO WILLINGLY CHOOSE TO BE INTERRUPTED EVERY TEN SECONDS

Can you name one profession where folks are overqualified and overworked, but also underappreciated and underpaid? If you guessed *public school teachers*, you are right!

As a parent, I know how hard raising a child can be. I'm so grateful to those who willingly choose a profession that requires raising hundreds of kids, none of whom are their biological children. There can be no explanation for this other than that these folks are simply amazing humans.

More often than not, when you ask a successful person to name people who played pivotal roles in their childhood or life, a teacher's name is bound to pop up.

At least back in the day, helicopter parents weren't that common. Take my dad, for example. Whenever someone asked him what grade I was in, he'd call me in, introduce me to the person asking the question, and then have me answer it myself. He said he was training me to be independent. I now know the truth—he could never remember what grade I was in. To him, it was inconsequential. What mattered was that I was in a good school under the tutelage of capable teachers.

Thanks to a comfortable and stress-free childhood, most of my memories have all blended into a collective mush that makes recalling specific instances difficult. But I remember my teachers all the way from elementary to high school. (Unfortunately, college teachers . . . not so much, because, to be quite honest, making attendance optional wasn't such a great idea.)

I'm especially fond of my late English teacher, a nun at the convent I attended. She nurtured my reading habit, always asking me what I was reading outside of school. She helped me appreciate *Oliver Twist* and *A Tale of Two Cities* (for some reason, Dickens dominated our curriculum).

She taught us about using *bombastic* words (sparingly) for dramatic effect. I took it to heart then and I'm still reminded of this lesson today. When I use a word with more than three syllables in a conversation or presentation, I notice an element of surprise in my audience. I credit this to their cognitive bias. As a brown woman with an accent, it's like they don't expect me to use complicated words. I get a kick out of it.

ANCIENT EASTERN TRADITIONS venerate the teacher (*guru*). "*Mata, pita, guru, deivam*" is a well-known traditional Sanskrit phrase that defines the order of importance of various roles in a person's life; in other words, a hierarchy.

The most important person in a child's life is her mother (*Mata*), followed by her father (*Pita*), then her teacher (*Guru*), and finally, God (*Deivam*). The theory is that a child innately knows their mother, the mother guides the child toward the father, the father leads the child to their teacher, and the teacher shows the child the path to the ultimate realization.

Lesson: Underestimate the importance of teachers at your peril. Deep. I know!

THEREFORE, it was quite natural for me to include a teacher as part of this project. I picked a teacher from my child's new class. Because of the pandemic, I'd never met this teacher since the school was in distance-learning mode.

I emailed her, thanked her for her service, and asked for a way to send her a small donation. I did not hear back that day. Or the next. Then, I went into an overthinking mode and agonized over my decision. Would I be causing a conflict of interest by offering a donation? Or heaven forbid, what if she thought I was trying to buy my child a grade?

Since I grew up in a society where bribery and corruption ran rampant, these fears were quite natural and real. By day three, after I hadn't heard from the teacher, I felt better about my teacher's silence. The story I told myself was that she understood I was on shaky ethical ground and by ignoring my email, she was going to forgive my transgressions. Phew! An easy way to get out of the hole I had dug for myself.

I planned to pick another teacher. Someone who had taught my child previously or, better still, a random teacher in another state—once bitten, twice shy!

Then, the email came from my child's teacher. She said it was sweet that I offered to donate. I immediately took the opportunity to clear up any confusion. I told her she could refuse if she felt there could be a conflict of interest. Then, she asked me if I had a child in her class.

Ah! It was then it dawned on me that the teacher had no way of knowing who I was. *Sweeeet!* I hadn't used my child's first or last name in the conversation, and my email address was fairly anonymous. Perfect.

I told the teacher I had a child in one of her classes, but that I'd prefer to stay anonymous. I told her I'd love to meet her one day and thank her in person. She teaches multiple grades of large class sizes, so I knew it would be impossible for her to find out.

Ultimately, it worked out well. I thanked the teacher profusely on behalf of parents worldwide. I may have gushed a bit. It was email, after all, and I was a practically anonymous person. So, I piled on the praise. It was genuine, but I wouldn't have been able to say all of that face-to-face, lest she should think I was some nutcase. She probably thought it anyway; oh, well!

I was happy, hiding behind my newfound anonymity and for making a teacher's life just a smidge better. Win-Win.

DAY 8: TRASH

WHEN THE GARBAGE GOES OUT MORE THAN YOU DO

I had decided whom to stalk next for the Giving Project: the trash truck driver. Could you think of someone more deserving? Rain or shine, they are out week after week, clearing out overflowing trash cans. Without sanitation workers, our lives would be full of—you guessed it—trash! No doubt about that.

Especially with the pandemic and shelter-in-place orders, the garbage was undoubtedly getting out more than me. And these truck drivers continued to be kind enough to give the bags a ride. I resolved to give back to them as part of the Giving Project.

So, on trash pickup day in my neighborhood, I woke up filled with excitement . . . but equally with dread. This particular act of giving would take a degree of logistical masterminding I didn't have to bother with until now. I had multiple factors to balance here.

My desire to keep this project a secret from my family meant I had to find a way to flag down the truck driver away from my street. My reluctance to do this in front of other neighbors also meant I had to find a quiet street. And somehow, I needed to find a way to be in the right place at the right time—that is, when the truck was coming down that quiet street! It seemed all too hard; I have a newfound respect for detectives and the police.

The last time I remembered someone being as fascinated with trash trucks as this was years ago—when I was a parent volunteer in my child's first grade class. One of the kids, Jake, was completely enamored by trash trucks. It was Career Day, and he said he wanted to grow up to drive one of those trucks. He waxed eloquent (for a six-year-old) about the joys of the garbage truck.

I found myself looking forward to the garbage truck driving into our neighborhood with as much anticipation as Jake probably does each week on trash day.

I went for a run early, hoping to *run* into the truck. I ran a few miles, in loops, on neighborhood streets instead of around the park as I usually do. As luck would have it, miles went by, but the truck didn't show up. Exhausted, I headed back home, showered, and waited, listening for sounds of the truck.

I hadn't appreciated it before, but on that day, I was glad for the loud, grating sounds these trucks make. I listened intently for those. (I have since discovered that there are phone ringtones that emulate garbage truck sounds. I'm guessing Jake now has a job creating ringtones.)

Finally, I heard it. I picked up the cash and my mailbox keys and headed out while my husband looked at me quizzically? Mail? At 8:45 a.m.? I told him I was expecting something important and hadn't checked the mail yesterday. Phew! That's what you call thinking on your feet.

Then I ran out onto the street—now in my flip flops, of course, and not my running shoes. I looked around to make sure no neighbors were watching. The truck driver seemed to be playing a game of cat and mouse with me. I walked back and forth, hoping to intercept him, but each time I thought he was headed my way, he turned a corner and disappeared out of sight. I finally just waited for him to show up on a side street. Patience has never been one of my virtues, and it was being put to the test.

Finally, the truck approached; I stood by a trash can and waved at him. I could see the annoyance on his face. He probably thought I was waiting to complain about something. What other reason would you have for flagging down a garbage truck driver? Certainly not to exchange pleasantries or discuss the weather.

He lowered his window. Without wasting time, I reached up to his window and handed him the money. It was a funny sight if there ever was one. The truck driver seated in a very tall truck and me, all of five foot four (on a good day), reaching up. I told him I was grateful for what he did. He seemed genuinely surprised, smiled, said "thank you," and drove away.

I SMILED ALL the way back home like I had carried out a *coup d'etat* and overthrown a communist government!

Thanks to the endless Zoom calls that defined our work-from-home routines during the pandemic, my husband didn't notice that I walked empty-handed back into the house with no mail.

That kid, Jake, was right. Truck drivers are indeed cool. I also had a personal growth lesson. With a little motivation and effort, you can achieve anything—even stop a dumpster truck for a few minutes!

DAY 9: PLAN C

SOMETIMES OPPORTUNITY COMES KNOCKING. LITERALLY.

I started the day wanting to tip the mailman. The trouble with that plan, I knew, was going to be catching him in time. After all, the whole mail delivery business model runs on the principle of *get-in-get-out-quickly*.

I live in a neighborhood with shared community mailboxes peppered throughout the community, so my mailbox is on a different street than my house. I've given up trying to figure out my mailman's schedule. I don't know if it's deliberate or an accident, but my mailman always delivers mail *after* my daily trip to the mailbox, seemingly no matter when I go. I think it's a running joke in his head.

I paced back and forth between my house and the mailbox a couple of times in the morning. Then I realized I was acting weird and a little too eager. I've read one too many stories about middle-aged women's fascination with mailmen! Anyway, after a few unsuccessful attempts, I headed back to my desk in search of Plan B.

That's when I read online about the rules for tipping government workers, such as mail carriers. Apparently, each household can only tip them twenty dollars a year. What?! Of course, the omnipotent worldwide web was full of articles about how such an archaic rule shouldn't stop one from doing the right thing. How would anyone know if you tipped them more, these articles asked. I agreed.

Then my overthinking brain went into overdrive. What if I did tip my mailman over the legally recommended amount? What if the government later finds out about it because I was stupid enough to write about it here? Then, what if both the mailman and I get penalized for attempted bribery and corruption? And so on.

So, I stopped looking for the mailman. As a side note, if you ever need examples of logical fallacies in thinking, reach out to me. I have enough to fill a book.

I did the next best thing. I quickly went to the USPS website and ordered stamps to show support for their mission. Never mind that I can't remember the last time I mailed a letter out. But this seemed to be a quick and easy way to assuage my guilt. Anyway, this is why the mailman did *not* become a part of the Giving Project. Now I needed a Plan C.

Serendipitously, a couple of minutes after my stamp-buying exercise, I received an email notification from my neighborhood social media app. If you aren't familiar with neighborhood apps, I will say they have some benefits, such as getting recommendations for handymen or plumbers. The app, though, is primarily a medium for self-appointed neighborhood vigilante to shame folks who don't pick up after their dogs or to air outrage about similar issues. In true social media style, things you'd never say to another person's face get aired on the app. It gets old. Fast.

So, unless I'm looking for someone to repair a broken cabinet or fix a leaky pipe, I rarely open up the app or bother with the email notifications. This time, though, the subject line of the notification email caught my attention. It said, "Family in need of urgent help." I don't know if you call this serendipity, dumb luck, or divine intervention, but the world just created a perfect case of supply and demand.

A family with three kids had lost their primary income source and was struggling to get by. A friend of the family was requesting assistance. I did not have any connections to either the family or the person requesting assistance on their behalf.

Yes, I was worried it could be a scam, but some basic sleuthing around in the app convinced me the poster was genuine. And she didn't seem to partake in outrage campaigns such as the one I had discussed earlier (i.e., I did not see any comments from her reprimanding folks for leaving their garbage bins outside their house after trash pick-up day). That sealed the deal for me. I let her know that I'd like to offer some financial help to the family in need. She gave me the details. Within a few minutes, I sent her some money.

I had just given away money to help a faceless, nameless person. Unlike other instances where I had some personal connection to the cause, this time my giving was to a complete stranger who I didn't seek out.

HAVING HAD the good fortune to live comfortably all through life, I've never really had to experience the pain of real financial struggles. But I could empathize and wonder what it would feel like not to know how to put food on the table. It was heart-breaking.

Knowing my humble contribution would make a small, positive difference in this person's life was comforting. Truth be told, hiding behind a wall of anonymity made this act of giving so much easier. I was back in my comfort zone. And I rationalized that was okay because it was to help a struggling family.

I know this sounds like esoteric talk, but the timing of the request for help could not have been more perfect.

> **I now believe this: when you care to do good, the universe conspires to make it happen.**

DAY 10: PACKAGES

MAKING SANTA LOOK LIKE A SLACKER

I'm attracted to productivity hacks like a moth drawn to light. One of my favorite activities is finding ways to optimize time. My love for "efficient action" is so deep that I'm sure there's a Latin-worded syndrome for it. I'll get someone to psychoanalyze this tendency later—don't have time right now for it.

This desire to do the most I can in the least amount of time led me to embrace online shopping in its infancy. Even when Amazon was just the "Earth's largest bookstore," I tried to buck the trend of visiting brick-and-mortar stores. Instead, I tried to find online marketplace equivalents for items I wanted to buy. I didn't care about the visual and tactile experiences of buying. I reckoned those were for people who had time to waste.

Fast forward to today, of course, and I'm no longer in the minority with my preference for digital shopping experiences. Yes, I shop for mundane items online—kitchen paper towels, office supplies, batteries. But I don't stop there.

The extent to which I shop online would undoubtedly give even veteran online shoppers some pause. Appliances? Check. The entire family's wardrobe, shoes included? Check. Large furniture, sight unseen? Check. I've probably visited the local mall exactly twice in the last year (and that was pre-pandemic)—and that was just to return online purchases.

The people that bear the brunt of my shopping predilection are the folks whose job it is to bring those packages to me—boxes of all sizes and shapes, constantly. So, quite naturally, I wanted to include a delivery person in the Giving Project.

AS DESCRIBED EARLIER, my attempts at tracking down my mail carrier was a flop—it turned out to be more difficult (and less legal) than I imagined. So, I pivoted to private couriers/package delivery services. I could freely tip these drivers. But to stay on track for my twenty-one–day challenge, I had to find one soon.

Then I lucked out. I had a scheduled package delivery from Amazon. I got excited! Not for the package itself—dish soap—but for the opportunity to pay back one of the delivery workers. I wasn't going to miss an opportunity that literally presented itself at my doorstep. The trouble, again, was in timing the arrival of the delivery.

Allow me to rant here for a bit about the concept of *notifications* or *alerts*. Most of us innocently click through an *Allow notifications* checkbox when we sign up for online services. As a consumer, all we care to know are answers to two questions.

1. Will I get the product?

2. What is the ETA?

But before we know it, we are ***inundated*** instead of just being *notified*. We get alerted when someone gets off their chair to pick up the order slip, when they put on their shoes, when they locate the bin number that our item sits in, when they put it in a box, and so on. Every single one of these events is timestamped and relayed to us. I can tell you my parents didn't even record the birth of their children with such gusto.

As a savvy consumer, therefore, I typically turn these notifications off. I have a conspiracy theory, though: when you turn notifications off, you anger some influential people. Consequently, you'll soon experience a delayed shipment. Let's say for coffee beans or shampoo. You panic, because that's what you do when your *just-in-time* inventory management system for coffee fails. Missed shipments, coupled with the reluctance to set foot in a store, makes you turn the notifications back on. Eventually, your coffee package arrives, but you forget to turn the notifications off. See how they get you? Now, the alert gods are happy and go back to cluttering your inbox with irrelevant updates.

Anyway, the point here is that I had my step-by-step delivery notification feature turned **on** this time. Not only did I get two reminders early in the day that my package would be delivered, but by mid-afternoon, they started a countdown timer. It felt like the New Year's Eve ball drop at Times Square. The alert said, *See where your package is on the map. Only ten stops away.*

The excitement was killing me. (That's sarcasm, by the way—a writer's nightmare. Almost like telling people after the fact that what you said was a joke. Pitiful.)

Excitement notwithstanding, I started pacing outside the house. It was weird. I'm in America. People typically leave their homes in their cars; rarely are they on their feet. The last time I saw neighbors walking on the street was when we were threatened by a fast-moving forest fire nearby. People walked over to the corner lot to get a sense of where the fire was heading—to check when they needed to get into their cars.

Finally, the Amazon delivery truck showed up. As the delivery man walked up to the house, he was busy looking down at his scanner. Unsurprisingly, when he looked up, he was startled to see me on the driveway. (It recently dawned on me that this project's entire plot is not that much different from a creepy serial killer movie's plot. What with all the planning, surprising people, and nervousness. I guess I'm glad this is about giving rather than taking.)

Nonetheless, after receiving the package, I handed the delivery person the money I had been holding in my hand. He said, and I quote, "What? I can't take that." I told him it was merely a small token of appreciation. He stood there in disbelief, trying to return it to me. I started panicking because I didn't want anyone inside the house to hear our conversation. I told him I was handing out cash to everyone that day, just to thank folks for their hard work during a difficult time. Smooth? Not so much. He probably sensed the desperation in my voice and took the money to end our conversation. He seemed grateful, and confused.

After he left, I walked in and closed all the shutters right away—as you do—glad to have checked off another day!

DAY 11: SANITY

THE SECRET TO A HAPPY MARRIAGE: A HOUSE-CLEANING SERVICE

*H*ere's a fact, not an opinion: outer order leads to inner calm.

I understood this very early on, thanks to my mother's insistence on "a place for everything and everything in its place." It's safe to say I've lived sorting life into neat, little piles—keep, donate, throw away. Strangely enough, not everyone embraces this fact. Or, at least, people pretend they don't understand so that others can pick up after them.

There are two types of people in this world: those who pick up after themselves and those who don't. The former group is always trying to convert the latter into their fold. Sadly, that never works.

I always thought cleaning was fun. I have distinct memories of my early teen years, when my parents would sometimes go to dinner parties and leave us kids at home with grandparents. I'd spend the time in a Zen-like state, listening to music while organizing all the cushions and lining up removable sofa-covers *just so*. Yes, I was that dork. I guess I didn't have anything better to do. And it felt good.

Growing up is challenging in so many ways, especially when responsibilities sneak up on you. One day you are responsible for keeping just your room clean (and sofa covers if you were me). Before you know it, you have a whole house, all your possessions, and your kids (and their possessions) to keep organized! Paradoxically, that's when your job, parenting duties, and other grown-up responsibilities vie for your attention, too.

That's the predicament I found myself in. As the years went by and my family and our possessions grew, I noticed a large part of my non-work time consumed with cleaning, sorting, and putting things away.

I once read motivational speaker and productivity expert Jim Rohn's words, "Don't major in minor things." I wouldn't be surprised if he wrote those words after seeing someone like me flitting around their house, spending their only "free" time, cleaning.

Just when I thought I'd put everything away and got it all done, another day would dawn—dust started to build up, possessions went jaywalking around the house, and clutter made its scheduled appearance. I'd feel compelled to start the tidying-up process all over again. And again. It didn't help that I'm married to someone who believes that the urge to clean is a feeling that will eventually pass if you just take a nap or distract yourself with something else.

As jobs and other responsibilities (not to mention the square footage of the houses we lived in) grew, cleaning marathons consumed my weekends. Faced with this fact, I had a choice. Should I continue to prod on or was it time to get help?

It is a question I struggled with on so many levels. I grew up in India, a place, where it's quite natural, even today, for most people to have assistance in running their household. But decades after migrating to the *do-it-yourself* Western world, let's say I've had my share of cultural immersion (*brainwashed?*) into thinking that getting household help is a clear admission of one of two things. Either you're too shabby to keep your own surroundings clean or you consider yourself too privileged to pick up stuff off your own floors. A no-win situation, because, really, no one likes to be labeled filthy or be riddled with guilt.

All that said, because my mental sanity was at stake, I finally gave in. Haters gonna hate.

Self-care, for some, involves spa trips or retail therapy. For me, it is a clean house—no doubt about that. For my sanity and those around me, I figured that hiring professional cleaners to keep the house clean periodically was my ticket to keeping the family peace.

Hiring someone to clean your house feels, in some ways, about as tricky as baring your soul to a therapist. You're essentially allowing someone to see the good, the bad, and the ugly. So yes, to tone down the ugly, I, like most people, *pre-clean* (a tad) before my cleaner shows up. When I hear someone say that's just redundant and stupid, I know they have never cleaned a day in their lives. To me, pre-cleaning is as natural as putting a raincoat on before stepping into the rain. You'll still get wet, but at least you protect your expensive suit. Similarly, the cleaner will still judge you, but at least you show her you put in some effort into maintenance after her last cleaning session.

Therefore, it was a no-brainer to include my house cleaner in the giving project—an easy option—both in terms of decision and execution. I cannot overstate the value and freedom the cleaner has added to my life. I started a practice of maintaining a gratitude journal a few years ago. When I review those journals, I can see, like clockwork, every couple of weeks, how thankful I'm when the cleaner visits my house. There are few things that lift my soul like the sight of gleaming, smudge-free hardwood floors.

For the Giving Project, I simply handed my cleaner some money in addition to her usual check when she came in. She probably will never realize how invaluable her services are to my sanity!

Also, by far, this was the easiest of the twenty-one days for me. No awkwardness or nervousness on my part. No pit in my stomach or stepping outside my comfort zone. Easy-peasy!

DAY 12: SAINTS

IF YOU CANNOT FEED A HUNDRED PEOPLE, FEED JUST ONE

When I started the Giving Project, I knew I was stepping outside my emotional comfort zone. I've always known I'm privileged to be living the life I do. Still, like many others in my situation, I cloak myself in an invisible layer of denial to avoid confronting just how difficult life can be for others.

Every so often, that layer gets punctured. Sometimes a little, sometimes a lot. Just as a punctured tire causes all the air to gush out, perforations of the privilege bubble cause feelings of guilt, deep anguish, and pondering about the unfairness of life to surface. Empathy is too nice a word to use in such situations. There is a rawness to the feeling that cannot be sugarcoated.

Strangely enough, I encountered such starkness not through an in-person giving situation, but through an online donation. A friend collects contributions locally and sends them over to India, where she has an associate doing some incredibly meaningful work with feeding the hungry. For the sake of anonymity, I'm merely going to refer to the associate as

TAKE MY MONEY, PLEASE

Asha. An apt moniker because *Asha* means hope—that's truly what she embodies.

It's not new, nor is it news to give money to charities that feed the hungry. There are NGOs, nonprofits, and companies working to fight these issues, but they can only accomplish so much without people in the community helping their neighbors.

Then there are some in the community who take on outsized roles to serve others selflessly. There is no quid-pro-quo involved here. They give because they realize there's an opportunity to make someone else's life better. Period.

I WAS INCREDIBLY lucky to be connected with one such person—Asha. I don't know her personally, but my friend shared some pictures of her work. She works tirelessly, day in and day out, to get food, groceries, supplies, and medical help to those in need. Not for recognition, but entirely out of the goodness of her heart.

People like her make it easy for people like me to donate. We do the easy part; she does the incredibly hard work of finding the needy and making sure to meet their needs.

While the giving process itself was easy, I wasn't prepared for the guilt after seeing some of the pictures of her work. There was a picture of a malnourished boy looking fondly at a plate of food. That image just tugged the strings of my heart. Again, these are pictures we've all seen millions of times. But when it's of someone who's only a couple of degrees of separation from you, it makes it all the more real. It did not take long for my denial bubble to be punctured. I felt deflated, but also hopeful to know there are *Ashas* everywhere to assist people who are willing to help but don't quite know how to.

I knew my small contribution would help someone like this young boy for a few meals. But then what? I wasn't sure. I do know this, though: with more *Ashas* out in the world to rescue humans from the throes of poverty and hunger, the world will be a better place. It's our choice to become *Ashas* ourselves, or to facilitate their work through giving.

DAY 13: INNER PEACE

IT'S NOT WHAT YOU THINK

I draw ire from people when I do this, but I can't help myself: I like to categorize people. Neatly. Into opposites. Lazy/hardworking, funny/annoying, selfish/selfless, and so on. Many people hate such abject categorizations. I have a category for those as well—haters/don't-carers. The haters tell me I'm dead wrong. *Everyone lives in the grey,* they say; *I shouldn't silo them into black/white.*

Well, maybe. But I do it anyway.

Here's the thing, though. I'm a simple person. I like putting people in boxes sometimes. Politically incorrect as it may sound, the way I do it is quite harmless. At least I think so. Usually, it's just me judging people in situations. Yeah, yeah— I know I shouldn't be making any judgments. Thankfully, over time, I've learned to keep these ideas in my head to avoid too many repercussions. In other words, as I've aged, I've learned to keep my trap shut. Somewhat.

I remember an incident a couple of decades ago when my family lived in New Zealand. I had invited some folks over for dinner at home. One conversation led to another. Before long, I went on a tirade about the injustice of India's British colonization, the lingering effects of oppression on the country, and other such topics. To say I was on a roll would be an understatement. There was no stopping me. I waxed eloquent about how the British monarchy *stole* the Kohinoor diamond. I acted like my family's heirloom was wrongfully pried from my hands. As usual, I was putting people into cut-and-dry boxes: Indian/Non-Indian; right/wrong.

All this invective was directed at my poor dinner guests, most of whom had British ancestry. Here I was feeding them dinner on the one hand and seemingly admonishing them on the other. They nodded politely. What choice did they have? They were Kiwis—the friendliest people on the face of the earth. They probably had never given any thought to India's colonization troubles. And they were too polite to interrupt my "woke" speech—this was years before *wokeness* as a term or even a concept existed. It's a testament to the good nature of these folks that we remain friends to this day.

The good news is that such cringe-worthy moments in my life have become few and far between over the years. I guess that's what they call wisdom (*knowing tomato is a fruit, but not putting it in a fruit salad*).

It's here that I'd like to correct a common misperception. Age, by itself, doesn't magically make you wiser. Age simply makes you older; wisdom comes when you learn from experience and modify behavior accordingly. I've seen enough *old children*—old in age but with child-like maturity—to know this as the truth.

My meditation practice gets a lot of credit for turning me from clueless to not-so-clueless. I'm not going to spend too much time extolling the virtues of meditation here; there's enough evidence online for you to read.

In a nutshell, though, meditation is a practice that allows you to withdraw your senses from being carried away by the endless distractions in the world. It helps you recognize the present for what it is. If the benefits of meditation were available in pill form today, it would be the number one drug on the planet.

Meditation helps you learn the skill of putting a giant pause button between trigger and response. The more you meditate, the more calmly and mindfully you can react in the moment to a tense or stressful situation. When your eyes see something and your mouth wants to respond, a meditation practice can help you control your overeager mouth to allow the brain to filter your response. Why wouldn't the world want more of this?

Meditation doesn't just help avoid gaffes or cringe-worthy moments. Emotions such as anxiety, overthinking, panicking can be curtailed, to a large extent, through the practice of meditation.

I went looking for a meditation teacher at a particularly bleak time in my life, riddled with anxiety. My choices were to try meditation first and if that didn't work out, then on to therapy and prescription meds. I found a local meditation group and an engaging and excellent teacher who introduced me to the art of meditation. The results were life-changing. And that's not hyperbole.

Consequently, I have managed to find time to schedule a mindfulness practice almost daily. I'm certainly not an enlightened being—far, far from it. But I'm much less scatterbrained and more self-aware than before. That, my friends, is a huge win, not just for me but for the world.

IN THIS CONTEXT, giving back to the meditation teacher was an easy choice for me. However, with the pandemic in place, local meditation groups aren't meeting like they used to. The silver lining is that these sessions are online now. So, I didn't have to go through a dog and pony show to make my donation.

The meditation tradition relies on voluntary *Dana* (donation) to teachers since the sessions themselves are usually free.

I'm grateful for both the practice and the opportunity to give back to my teacher.

By giving, I gained something much more valuable—inner peace.

DAY 14: FIREFIGHTERS

WHAT THE BRAVEST GO ON TO BECOME

When I accepted a job offer that required me to move to California years ago, I was quite excited. I had visited the Golden State before but was quite thrilled at the prospect of becoming a resident. There was no shortage of attractions—natural or human-made. In just a few hours, I could go from the pristine beauty of Lake Tahoe to the magnificence of towering Yosemite or the bustle of Disneyland and the bling of Hollywood. You'd be hard-pressed to find this kind of diversity in terms of people or landscapes anywhere else in the world.

Higher taxes seemed worthwhile when weighed against eternal sunshine and the ability to be outdoors most of the year. I'm an avid runner, yet I've never owned a treadmill because running outside is always my preferred option. For that, I'm grateful to California.

So, after a decade of leading a somewhat nomadic lifestyle, residing in ten cities across three continents, I found *home* in California. Sadly, something that has proliferated during this time is the number of ravaging state-wide wildfires. Nature has been very keen to prove who is in charge.

Year after year, the scenes from the wildfires are apocalyptic. Yes, California has always been at high risk of fires. But the ten most massive wildfires in the States have occurred here in the very recent past.

A few months ago, I had personal experience with just how terrifying an ordeal like this can be. It seemed business as usual on a weekday, but then we were alerted to a nearby, quick-moving grass fire. We continued working, assuming the fire was still miles away. Then we heard the sound of fire trucks.

I stepped outside my house to see what was going on—two things completely blew my mind. The acrid smell of smoke hung in the air, and there was low visibility outside, even though it was 2 p.m. on what had started as a bright, cloudless summer day. Before we could get a sense of what was going on, we had four fire trucks line up just across our street. They said they were guarding the perimeter and would have to break down the community fences to let us drive through, should the need arise.

We were soon packing up our possessions and making judgment calls on what belongings were valuable enough to be saved. We had accumulated stuff over fifteen years of living in California—now, we had fifteen minutes to decide which of those items made the cut. Just the prior week, we had replaced our carpets. I couldn't help but longingly look at our new carpets and think what a waste that was. Anyway, dazed, we packed what we could and were ready to bolt if the orders came.

While I was busy debating whether my favorite book was worth saving, there were some extraordinarily selfless and brave men and women battling the fire a few miles away, trying to contain it from moving into population centers such as ours. We were fortunate enough that they were able to contain the fire before it reached our neighborhood. This fire had destroyed eight hundred acres of land and burned two structures to the ground, but our community was safe. We were just two miles away from carnage. It took a hundred firefighters to contain the fire. Freeways had been closed. Life had come to a standstill for a lot of people during that hour. Except for the firefighters.

The four fire trucks stationed across our street made their way back out after receiving the all-clear. The firefighters waved and honked; they had just averted disaster. Overwhelmed with gratitude, we went back to the comfort of our home.

They, on the other hand, didn't. Because there was now a new fire forty miles away. Another crisis was brewing, and more lives and property were in potential danger and required saving. Such is the life of a firefighter.

GIVEN ALL OF THIS, I knew I had to have a firefighter on this list. I was fortunate to find someone most-deserving. Let's call him Dave. His story is heartbreaking.

Dave had lost a child a year earlier. To raise his two other children, he had just bought a foreclosed property in the country. Dave was out on duty fighting a fire in the area, only to find out later that his newly purchased property had burned down in the same fire. What's worse, the insurance paperwork hadn't yet been completed on the property. Dave had just seen his dream end up in the rubble.

Thankfully, the local community stepped up with a fundraiser, hoping to help him rebuild the house of his dreams for his family. I was grateful to have the opportunity to pitch into this effort in a small way.

No monetary donation can compensate for the selfless service rendered by Dave and his fellow firefighters. It makes me cringe to think of the times I complained about poor coffee at work or how my chair wasn't ergonomic enough. In comparison, firefighters run the risk of losing their lives while on duty, not to mention their possessions.

It is one thing to be fighting a human-made problem; we can usually find a way to get out of the pickle we create for ourselves. However, when nature shows us she's the boss, there's not much you can do other than send some valiant firefighters out to fight their hardest.

As I wrote this, I had family in another part of California safely evacuated from their homes in response to a massive nearby wildfire--thanks to the firefighters. Again.

DAY 15: PERSPECTIVE

IF YOU CAN'T PAY IT BACK, PAY IT FORWARD

One day you're going about your life complaining about the littlest things. Dishes left on the kitchen counter instead of the sink, someone cutting you off on your drive, or a web page taking too long to load.

And then, you hear about it: someone you know gets a cancer diagnosis. You stop in your tracks. Your reaction is proportional to how close your connection to this person is. It's heartbreaking when it's someone you know personally. Devastating if it's a friend or family member.

You get a feeling that maybe you're fretting about the wrong things. Life is short. Perspective makes a brief appearance.

Three people I know have received a cancer diagnosis in the last twelve months. As a cancer survivor myself, I know what that feels like. When you hear the words, "you have cancer," just like that, ninety-nine percent of the things you were worried about a minute ago simply fall to the wayside.

The ancient Hindu Vedic scriptures use a Sanskrit term —*ekagrata*. It means one-pointedness: single-minded attention to a cause. The scriptures encourage cultivating *ekagrata* as a means toward attaining self-realization. They acknowledge it is difficult to nurture this practice because we are bound by numerous distractions all the time.

When someone informs you of a cancer diagnosis, you understand intuitively what *ekagrata* means, albeit in the wrong context. Because, at that moment, there is a realization that nothing else matters. Your existence is at stake. Never mind the fact that this is not what the scriptures recommend you single-pointedly reflect upon, but your life as you know it—with all its whims and fancies, do's and don'ts, ups and downs—is now in jeopardy. It's like you're staring at an abyss.

I CANNOT OVERSTATE the helplessness people feel in the face of a cancer diagnosis. We all have different ways of processing such news in terms of how long we remain stunned or how quickly we move on. But, one thing is for sure: the sucker-punch to the gut that such diagnoses bring with it is real. And painful.

There is *one* primary root cause for all that pain and suffering: fear. Fear of the unknown. It's like you have spent your entire life carefully building your dream home, brick by brick. Now, abruptly, you find out the only brick-supplying company is closing down. You don't know if there will ever be a supply of bricks in the world again. You worry about the half-built house, considering the sweat and equity that has already gone into it. Some truly existential concerns cross your mind.

EVERY DAY, there are about five thousand new cancer diagnoses in the world. Of course, this number is much larger if you take into account other severe and terminal illnesses. That's five thousand people *plus* all their loved ones who take this heartbreaking journey staring at the abyss and wondering what'll happen to their brick-homes. Every. Single. Day.

While I don't know if or when there'll be a cure for cancer or if we will ever be able to entirely prevent cancer, I'm sure we can soften the dread of a cancer diagnosis by replacing fear with hope. It need not be all doom and gloom. We're in the twenty-first century, after all. Medical treatments have evolved a lot more from the days when leeches roamed human bodies to suck diseased blood out, or physicians removed whole body parts and organs to stop disease from spreading.

For hope to replace dread, cancer research and support groups need funding assistance. When a family gets a cancer diagnosis, having professionals hold their hand and reassure them is always a better option than letting them fend for themselves through Google searches.

I understand some may think funding cancer research and support groups aren't a priority because they haven't been impacted personally. Unfortunately, I hate to be the bearer of bad news. Here are some statistics from cancer.org: on average, American men have a one in two risk of developing some cancer in their lifetimes, and American women have a one in three chance. Yes, it's that bad. Of course, your odds may be better or worse than the average, but these are some stark statistics. Not to sound morbid, but cancer is closer to you than you might think.

When I opened up my email and saw a friend requesting a donation to a three-day walk for a cancer support group, I did not hesitate. This deviated from one of the rules I had set for the Giving Project (about giving to individuals instead of institutions), but I figured I was helping *his* journey. With the pandemic in place and purses tightened, his fundraising was going slower than usual. Unfortunately, cancer doesn't stop for the pandemic.

Plus, the universe seemed to be sending me a message. It so happened, just a couple of days before the email, I had a long conversation with a friend who's still in cancer treatment. She's my age. We spoke on the phone and her anxiety was palpable, even though she tried to sound optimistic. She and I, and all her other loved ones, are helpless. By donating to organizations fighting cancer, we're doing something actionable to lessen this pain.

AS A SOCIETY, we need to find a way to tackle the feelings of helplessness in the face of life-threatening diagnoses. This cancer charity donation was one of the easier giving opportunities because it fell into my lap and checked off all the boxes that I'd check off anyway. And it felt good to give. I owe my very existence to the generous giving by so many that enabled me to get the treatments I needed. I was simply paying it forward.

DAY 16: THEORY OF MOTIVATION

MASLOW AND THE OVARIAN LOTTERY

American psychologist, Maslow, created one of the most famous pyramids (on paper; no threat to Giza) in modern times. His "Hierarchy of Needs" is a popular motivational theory to describe human behavior using five levels of motivation:

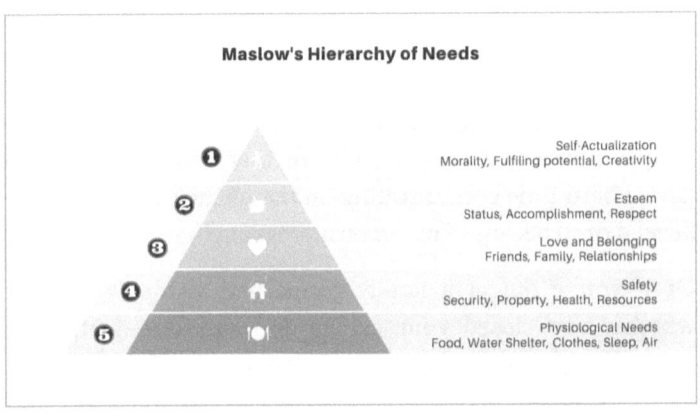

MASLOW'S THEORY OF HIERARCHY

In short, Maslow's theory is that we start at the bottom of the pyramid. We have little motivation to aspire to higher levels until needs at each level are met.

At the bottom of the pyramid are basic physical and psychological needs such as food, water, and shelter. The next level is for safety needs, paying one's bills, and having good physical health.

The third level is our search for belonging in terms of friendships, nurturing relationships, and family. The fourth is our motivation for recognition, yearning to be respected in the community, and the sense of accomplishment.

Finally, at the top level, we are motivated to search for the meaning of life and find ways to fulfill our potential on earth.

While popular, this theory has been debated quite widely. But then again, academicians like to debate. That's their thing.

Without putting too fine a point on it, we can safely assume the truth in the above theory. Suppose I forget to bring my jacket to an open-air lecture on the "purpose of life," and the temperature drops significantly. In that case, I'm going to have a hard time concentrating on the nuances of the lecture (level 4 or 5) because I'm too busy freezing (level 1).

Or if you're out at a family picnic and suddenly wonder whether you closed your garage door or turned off your stove (level 2), you are going to struggle to be the "life of the party" (level 3).

THIS LESSON in psychology wasn't merely about me showing off my knowledge of an academic theory.

In the years that I've lived in California, one problem that has been on the rise, rather severely, is homelessness. It is a divisive issue, as well, involving questions of personal responsibility. If we park politics to the side on this one, we can agree that this is a deeply distressing issue on a humanitarian level.

I'm not new to witnessing poverty and homelessness. I grew up in India, where the contrast between the rich, poor, and those in the middle has always been on full display for all to see. There is no escape from it.

That said, I'm not proud of how I reacted—or, to be accurate, did *not* respond—to the distress around me. I wasn't the only one with this *non-reaction* reaction. Most of us find coping mechanisms to deal with the associated guilt of watching the homeless. Sometimes we rooted ourselves in denial, while at other times, we tried to help out in whatever little way we could. We believed that this was a systemic problem requiring a large-scale effort, and we weren't going to solve it on our own.

In India, I witnessed a classic lesson on what happens when you don't nip an issue in the bud. The problems grow into monstrous proportions and overwhelm the system.

When I moved to America, ostensibly the land of opportunity and the world's leader in ensuring a minimum standard of living, it was a little shocking to find traces of the homeless issue I had seen so much of in India. Sadly, though, in the last few years, it isn't *traces of* homelessness anymore; this is now a burgeoning issue.

One of the amazing things about the human brain is how we *adapt* and don't let traumas or bad experiences keep us down forever. Unfortunately, this sort of adaptation is a double-edged-sword. If we keep *adapting* to the homeless issue, we may end up normalizing the situation and never actually addressing it.

Are you wondering how Maslow is relevant to the conversation about homelessness? (I told you I'd get to the point eventually.) Think of it like this: it's hard for a person who has no idea where his next meal is coming from or whether he'll have a warm blanket to tide him through rough weather, to worry about being a contributing member of society.

Our best bet to address this problem is to start at the ground level and make sure to rehabilitate the homeless in safe, loving surroundings. Most of us are too caught up in our own lives or too chicken to do that. But, we're lucky enough that there are saints amidst us who do just such a thing.

I FOUND some of them volunteering at the local homeless shelter. This organization is supported purely by the community and a few individuals and corporate donors, but with no reliance on any government assistance for their programs.

Volunteers at this shelter work tirelessly day in and day out, helping struggling folks meet the most basic needs, the lowest rungs of Maslow's hierarchy. These volunteers feed, clothe, and tend to the sick and imprisoned. They give a piece of themselves every day in the hope of recovering a part someone else has lost. There can be no greater service to humanity.

With social distancing rules in place, it was challenging to find an actual volunteer to give to, so instead, I donated to the shelter. Financial contributions are easy and appreciated. After I donated, I sat down and pondered something Warren Buffett (one of the wealthiest people in the world) had said before.

Buffet, arguably the world's best philanthropist, credits his financial success to luck. At the Berkshire Hathway's Annual Shareholder event in 2018, he said,

> "The ovarian lottery is the most important event in which you'll ever participate. It's going to determine way more than what school you go to, how hard you work, all kinds of things."

In other words, who you're born to (the ovarian lottery), and the emotional, social and financial circumstances of your birth, determine your life's path to a great degree.

By merely winning the ovarian lottery I was able to shortcut Maslow's hierarchy and get to level 4. I recognize the privilege I've had and how lucky I've been to have the opportunities I've had. As years have gone by and some semblance of wisdom has emerged, I know it would be a gross misuse and squandering of all that luck and goodwill bestowed on me if I don't pay it forward.

DAY 17: SELF-CARE

HOW TO BUILD SELF-CONFIDENCE: GET YOUR HAIR DONE

*A*t my all-girls school, only individuals belonging to one of these two groups were popular:

A) The uber-talented: The ones who got the lead role in school plays or were great orators or artists or good at sports.

B) The pretty ones: Their good looks were somehow obvious even through staid school uniforms. These girls were impeccably dressed, with hair that was never out of place, and confidence that could have only been generated from said outer perfection.

If you didn't belong to one of these categories, you were relegated to shadowing people in groups A and B like a swarm of bees. You simply blended into an indistinguishable collective cluster of faces and names.

And then, some of us were stragglers who didn't have the talent or the looks described above but we were also too proud to trail after the ones that did. Mostly we were what has come to now be known as *nerds*. Kind of. Sort of. Back then, we had a more forgiving term to describe my lot—*the thinking ones.*

As a member of *the thinking ones,* I never cared too much about my appearance. My vanity projects were (and to this day are) few and far between.

My universe consisted of my family, a few close friends, and books. It was a magnanimous space—usually, the only person criticizing me was myself. For that sheltered childhood, I'm grateful. As a result, I didn't particularly care about interacting with or trying to impress folks beyond my orbit. And if I did want to, I attempted to do it using the "small-talk about books" route rather than the "stun the room with your presence" route. That seemed to work for a bit, at least until young-adult insecurities took over.

The burden to up the ante in the looks category took hold in the local culture thanks to the advent of glam beauties in TV shows and mainstream media. I wasn't immune to this pressure and started to dabble with ways to go from drab to fab. It kept me busy for a while, you might say.

As I kept delving deeper into the quest for beautification, each attempt left me tired and exhausted. There seemed to exist an inherent conflict between my make-every-minute-count personality and the enormous time beauty regimens and skincare routines took.

But I noticed one area that seemed quite effortless. You see, I used to have a decent head of hair. (*Used to* being the operative phrase here.) Enough people had praised my mane growing up that I figured it was best to work with what I had —a decent head of hair. (By the way, working with what you have is a great life lesson for just about anything.)

My visits to the hairdresser became regular . . . but never became less awkward. I'm a hairdresser's worst nightmare because small talk and pleasantries don't come easily to me. Hairdressers try to engage with me, but after a few stilted attempts at conversation, they focus on their craft while I stare blankly into space, contemplating my to-do list.

Maybe it's this silence that lets the hairdressers focus on my hair, or perhaps they try their best not to have me come back any time soon. Regardless, the result is good for me because I always end up getting a great haircut. By the time I leave the salon, I feel like someone just gave me a shot of magic potion.

Who knew chopping a few layers of dead cells off could add a bounce to your step, a smile to your face, and a boost to your confidence? After a haircut, I always feel a kindred connection with the beauty queens from high school. For a few fleeting moments, at least.

Don't get me wrong. I'm someone who values character (and wit), and I have obvious disdain for the objectification of women. But I've also always understood one thing: though the purpose of some vanity projects may seem to be to impress others or get social media validation, they are almost like self-affirmations. In moderation, these vanity projects can have a feel-good quality about them. My life has gotten better since I embraced this philosophy.

Therefore, quite obviously, my giving list had to have a hairdresser on it. While the pandemic has awakened a DIY-mentality in many areas, some things should still be left to professionals. Cutting hair is one of them. You can try to DIY it, but in doing so, you may have to socially isolate yourself until your tresses grow back, even if the pandemic ended and the rest of the world is out and about.

Service workers, such as hairdressers, have been the worst hit during this time due to their reliance on gratuities. So, it was a no-brainer to tip my hairdresser generously. I caught her on a very busy day. She had a long line of customers (looking to fix disastrous quarantine haircuts, I presume) that needed her attention. She didn't have time for the usual chit-chat and so took the tip with a smile and said thanks. I was doubly-pleased—great haircut AND no awkward chit-chat.

Sometimes you can have your cake and eat it, too!

DAY 18: CLASH OF CULTURES

CAUGHT BETWEEN TWO WORLDS

A couple of birthdays ago, I had an epiphany. I was leafing through the puzzles section of a magazine and came across an age-related math (algebra) question. The ones that start like this: if Jill was three times as old as her son was five years ago and is now twice as old as her son is now . . . Yeah, one of *those* problems where you had to guess how old Jill is now.

A part of my brain blurted out the answer before I had a chance to read the question fully. The word that popped into my head was "old." I guess because it's a word that has become relatively common in my lexicon, making it easy to recall from my short-term memory.

Lately, I've had constant reminders of age creep up on me. It seemed like just a few months ago, I was the youngest person on my team at work. *An eager beaver,* they said. Now, I'm simply *wise counsel*—surrounded by *eager beavers*.

What happened? Where did the time go? But, more importantly, what's in store for me on the other side?

TAKE MY MONEY, PLEASE

∼

SPENDING equal parts of time between two cultures that view aging from a different prism has given me a unique perspective on the whole getting-old question.

For generations, Eastern cultures such as the one I grew up in embraced multigenerational households. Traditionally, countries in the East have had collectivist cultures, where the welfare of the group as a whole takes precedence over individual wellbeing.

I grew up in a historically patriarchal society. Revered family elders, usually men, made important decisions. While there may have been some rumblings and discontent, the will of the elders prevailed. Parents *and* grandparents (and half a dozen aunts and uncles) raised young children through to adulthood. It was then the turn of the newly minted adults to care of their aging parents and grandparents. There was plenty of give and take both ways.

This arrangement made sense because there was no external support or government-assisted social security net for families to rely on when they aged. Families spent whatever they could on raising and educating their children, with the unwritten and unspoken expectation that children would care for them when they age.

I guess this cycle continued for many generations until the advent of industrialization and urbanization. India's masses started to migrate to urban centers from a primarily agrarian society, leaving farms behind for factories.

The migration also meant a fracturing of the multi-generation household. While there was still an emphasis on maintaining family bonds and relationships, the concept of everyone being in everyone else's life all the time disappeared. The idea of *nuclear families* was born (a rather unfortunate term, in my opinion).

My generation is probably the first generations of kids raised in these nuclear families. I had various relatives, grandparents and great grandparents live with us for short periods over the years, but never had the constant presence of a family elder (other than parents) checking in on my whereabouts or whether I had done my homework[1].

The point is, influenced by my parents' reasonably independent lives, mine has been very independent as well. I left home for college at sixteen (no, I wasn't a genius—most people started college early. I guess parents were too fond of their newfound independence, so, they accelerated kids' learning to send them off to colleges when their kids' brains were still mush.)

Something that also changed with my generation was that we were no longer limited to domestic geographical limits. International emigration became a common thing.

Of course, in the beginning, a lot of people were enthusiastic. Parents were excited that their young adults were now living in countries with access to many opportunities that weren't available to them at home. The young adults were thrilled at the thought of participating in shenanigans so many miles away from their parents that they'd never get found out.

But a decade or so passed before the one constant in life—age—started to catch up to everyone. Parents began to face age-related issues just as their children were beginning to settle and have kids themselves.

Initially, people facing this issue used the approach I use to solve problems: bury your head in the sand and fervently wish that by the time you raise your head, the problem will have gone away. Sadly, that works about one in a million times.

Western societies have long embraced the independence model of sending kids off far and wide as soon as they can fend for themselves. However, they also accounted for the fact that the kids may not be able (or want) to return in time to take care of aging parents, leading to the advent of senior care homes and assisted living facilities.

In Eastern cultures, unfortunately, this didn't happen. In a rush to go from a collectivist to an individual society, folks realized a little too late that the cart had left before the horse was ready. Cultural expectations weren't reset, nor was there any talk of infrastructure development to deal with the brewing crisis of how to care for aging seniors in the absence of traditional support by younger family members.

Social taboos prevailed too strongly in most parts of the country even to suggest the idea of senior-care homes. It was considered almost inhumane by the majority of the population to leave aging family members by themselves. Several movies, daytime soap operas, and lecture series made this a central theme in their plotlines. As a result, there wasn't a significant push to even acknowledge the senior care gap until recent years.

Unfortunately, in the process, a genuine quandary has been created.

THE YOUNG ADULT, let's call him Kumar, who traveled overseas, hasn't just found higher education in the new country, but he has found his calling. It doesn't take long before

Kumar has a well-paying career, a growing family, and social and community ties in his newfound home.

Kumar is also governed by immigration laws that make it difficult, if not impossible, for him to unite his family. It is not easy to bring over his aging parents from his home country. While the immigration laws love Kumar's skills, age, and ability to contribute to society, the same laws have equal apathy to his parents' generation and their lack of "defined skills." And sometimes, rightly so, because the lawmakers are especially concerned about the drain Kumar's parents' generation could make on the country's medical resources, should they choose to emigrate.

Kumar now has the unenviable choice to either leave behind everything he created in the new land and move back to his home country *or* somehow find reliable assistance for his elderly folks back home. Unfortunately, neither are easy choices.

In the years since he has immigrated, Kumar has now adopted some of his new country's value systems that could conflict with the ones he grew up with as a child. Kumar's own children are now native citizens of the new land. It is a scary proposition for them to move to a country that is truly foreign to them.

While we can debate the morality and humanity of such situations, we must acknowledge the lack of an easy solution. It is what it is. Decisions have consequences. The decision Kumar and his parents made in their fit and healthy years now has a rather uncomfortable flip side.

Resulting, (very difficult) situations—, such as when Kumar has to give a work presentation right after a long-distance phone call with his terminally ill father living thousands of miles away—are all too commonplace. And heartbreaking. While straddling two equally dear worlds is tough for Kumar, not having the comforting presence of a loved child is harder on his father.

The inherent conflict between cultural values and reality can be quite distressing. These are uniquely twenty-first century problems, for sure, and they are painful.

NOW YOU KNOW why senior care centers are dear to me and why they have a special place in my heart. These centers run on the mission of looking after the welfare of senior citizens.

By giving to the senior care center, I was symbolically assuaging the guilt of a million Kumars and Kumaris. Workers and volunteers at these centers do the work that people like Kumar wish they could do with their own aging family members.

Let's not forget we wouldn't exist without our dear senior citizens.

Let's also not forget that we'll soon be them.

DAY 19: DINING OUT

YES, I SOMETIMES FAST. BETWEEN MEALS

I'm a foodie, born to a family of foodies, married to a foodie, and raising a foodie. I don't think I can possibly overstate the importance of food in my life.

Culturally, too, I come from a nation of gourmands. India is a large, vastly diverse country. Cities are paired with food and food with cities: Chennai *Idlis,* Amritsari *Kulchas,* Hyderabadi *Biriyanis,* Lucknowi *Kababs.*

Growing up amidst such a rich and varied food culture meant acknowledging the central role food played in our lives. The question, *"What's for dinner"* would surface as lunch plates were being cleared—and not for want of variety or quality at lunch. Light lunch is an oxymoron you'll never hear in India. If you don't believe me, Google the items on a *business lunch thali* option of any Indian restaurant.

Foods define religious festivities. Think Turkey at Thanksgiving, but multiply the number of options for each celebration by at least twenty. Food underlines all decisions.

TAKE MY MONEY, PLEASE

Back when I was making my college decision with my family, one of the factors influencing where I'd go to school was whether I had good food options either on or off-campus.

It's no surprise then, as I ventured out into the western world, that the thought of eating lettuce and ranch for lunch wasn't going to fly. But I made an effort to embrace eating uncomplicated foods. I tried to explain this over the phone to my grandmother back in India. (Yes, we talked about what was for lunch even on expensive long-distance phone calls.)

When I told her I'd had a Greek salad for lunch, she asked me about my other lunch courses. I told her the salad was it—the whole meal. Silence. Then she asked me if I was ill or on a restricted diet. I tried to convey a message about pursuing good health. I went on about food groups—carbs, fiber, fat. She said she needed to get off the phone to talk with my parents about letting me go to this food-forsaken land. *At what cost*, she wondered. Loudly.

So, it's no wonder I think of food constantly. My palate has expanded over the years, and with it also my understanding of nutrition and other aspects of food. But the importance of a good meal hasn't diminished for me.

Even my travel destinations are influenced by food choices. I wasn't thrilled when house rentals started to become the most popular travel lodging option, because that meant it was possible to make your own meals. Isn't it a travesty to cook on vacation? A few years ago, I thought I'd never see Galapagos Island in this lifetime given the lack of food choices there. Thankfully, that has changed now, making me believe more people on the planet weigh tourist attractions and availability of food choices at these destinations, on an equal scale.

Unsurprisingly, with the immersion training I got, I'm a decent cook. But like every other cook, I like to take breaks from cooking to patronize other chefs' culinary skills—both home chefs and the ones at restaurants.

As a cook, I know that the greatest joy isn't merely about creating a good meal. It's about being able to enjoy the meal without the thought of cleaning the stove or worrying about dishes to do. And for that, I'm eternally grateful to restaurants.

SOME OF THE hardest-hit folks in this pandemic are the service industry workers in restaurants, bars, coffee shops, and cafes. These service workers rely on gratuity for a significant portion of their income. The average amount Americans have spent on outside food in recent years has ranged from $3500 to $4500 per household, with about fifteen percent of that in gratuities.

According to estimates, spending on food dropped by almost fifty to seventy percent during to the pandemic. You don't have to be a math genius to figure out the massive income hit this pandemic has caused the food service industry.

All of this reflection of food and its oversized impact on my life got me thinking about how to incorporate restaurants into the Giving Project. It was a no-brainer for me to hand over a large tip when I paid for my takeout order. The person who served me looked perplexed when he saw the tip and wondered if I had miscalculated my payment. I sheepishly mentioned it was a small token of thanks. He still seemed confused but may have said thanks. I smiled, picked up my stuff, and hurried away before he said anything else.

It was the least I could do to thank those who feed us when we are either too lazy, inept, incapable of cooking ourselves.

DAY 20: MEDICAL DIARIES

WHY I TRIED TO ADOPT A NURSE

You hear of kids who find their passion early in life and work, laser-focused, toward their life dreams. These kids always knew how to answer the question "What do you want to be when you grow up?" Remarkably, their answer stayed the same year after year. I was always fascinated by these kids. But I wasn't one of them. I never knew what I wanted to be when I grew up. Truth be told, I still don't. I keep asking myself that question every so often. I come up empty most days.

That said, I was studious and academically proficient through my school years. I was told I needed to get good grades, so I did. But I never really nursed a passion for a subject or an idea. Yes, I'd be hit with waves of inspiration; but like real waves, they'd crash soon on the shore of reality, only to be replaced by another wave.

Thankfully, in high school, I was forced to choose between a science and an accounting program. I'm not sure if *I* made a choice to enroll in science or if the option was made *for me* by a combination of circumstances and family. In a way, this forced choice was right because it somewhat narrowed the field of college application choices.

I still applied to all sorts of science-based college programs—engineering courses, med schools, pure science studies. My progressive and forward-thinking parents also didn't let geographical considerations limit where I applied. So, there were a *lot* of applications sent out.

I was offered admission to and enrolled in a somewhat vague hybrid engineering/business program, albeit at a prestigious college. A couple of months after I started college, I got accepted to a top med school where I was previously waitlisted. My parents were thrilled—becoming a doctor is always a big deal. But then, I had to make another decision on whether I was going to switch.

Those two months I'd already spent at college seemed quite long to me. For someone who never made any decisions, this was a big one. I was quite happy to lay this at the feet of the universe. I reasoned, if I were meant for med school, I'd have been offered an admit at the beginning of my search. I decided to reject the med school offer and instead chose to stay put and finish the course I was already enrolled in, for the simple reason that I couldn't be bothered starting all over again. Case closed.

Quite honestly, I have not regretted that decision, especially seeing my med school friends spending nearly a decade in school and residencies, compared to my short and sweet four-year stint at college.

HERE's evidence to believe the theory that everything happens for a reason.

I had a good few years after college, followed by exciting career opportunities involving lots of travel. Then, my body simply went into rebellion. For someone who had a completely healthy childhood, save for a few bouts of cough and cold, I suddenly developed illnesses ranging from benign tumors and cysts to stage IV cancer.

That's when I figured if I had become a physician, I'd be too busy treating myself (patient zero) instead of others. Plus, I didn't need to attend medical school, after all, to learn medicine. As a subject of these treatments, I was getting a very practical education. Too bad they don't confer degrees on patients.

My trips to hospitals were frequent during this time. Not as a visitor, but a patient. With survival at stake.

Some of these trips I remember with fondness, such as when my daughter was born. I've tried to think less about other trips, such as the cancer center's infusion clinics. And then there were some surgeries. I can't remember much of those even if I wanted to, thanks to the power of anesthesia. There were also countless visits for lab draws, imaging, and other diagnostics. A nurse who drew my blood at my local hospital asked me once if I worked there because she said she'd seen me around before. No kidding. My commutes would have been more efficient had I simply picked up a job at the hospital.

Anyway, the underlying lesson I carry from all these health care visits is one of gratitude. I'm fit and healthy now thanks to work put in by the health-care professionals who treated me and those in the background—researchers, pharma companies, medical equipment makers, and so on. The list is endless.

Of all these workers, I have a special place in my heart for nurses. I have plenty of friends who are physicians, and in no way am I belittling their contributions. But the nurses—they are a gift to humanity.

Every single nurse I've had the privilege of dealing with (and as you can tell, there were MANY) has been incredible, without exception. I remember going through childbirth and feeling helpless, as first-time mothers do. The nurse on duty then was simply the most encouraging person I've ever met in my life.

Until that point, I hadn't been able to keep even a cactus plant alive. It was no surprise then that I was freaking out about birthing and then caring for a *baby*. The nurse assigned to me was a young woman but had a kind of ageless wisdom about her. She calmed me down and let me know I'd do fine. She comforted me and let me know all mothers started like this. I wasn't sure that was true, but it felt good hearing it.

Calmed, I wondered if I could adopt her as a second child. I may or may not have suggested this to her. I'm guessing she refused because we left the hospital with just our child—the one I had given birth to. I subsequently have attributed this to being loopy due to lack of sleep with a newborn.

That's how much I love nurses. Nursing is a job that requires empathy every minute while putting up with the whims and fancies of loopy patients. They don't get the option of simply walking away from a difficult problem as I do at work (just sometimes).

So, for the Giving Project, I tried to enlist a nurse recipient. But since this version 2.0 of me is much healthier, I don't have frequent visits to healthcare clinics (thankfully). With the pandemic in place, I realize medical staff also aren't generally waiting around to chit chat with me.

So, I found a good substitute option. I chose to give to a hardship fund for nursing students. To consider enrolling in nursing school is, in itself, an act of great sacrifice. I can't imagine how difficult it must be or such as student to be further inundated with a family illness or financial hardship in the pursuit of her education.

I hoped my tiny contribution finds its way to someone truly in need. The world cannot have enough caring nurses.

DAY 21: THE VERY END

THE NOT-SO-GRIM REAPER

Death is a subject we'd all rather not talk about. It's also a subject I prefer not to write about. As a matter of fact, my excuse is that I don't have first-hand experience (thankfully) to say too much about it.

So, this will be short.

For my twenty-first day of giving, I chose one of the noblest professions in the world—hospice care.

Given a choice, we all wish we could live until a ripe old age, party hard until the last day, and simply pass away in our sleep. Unfortunately, that experience is the exception rather than the norm.

To even opt for hospice care means a patient and their families have decided to forgo curative treatments. So, for most, it's rather a protracted battle between a spirit that may be ready to let go and a body that has almost but not quite given up.

In this fraught space, a hospice care worker tries to make the patient's life feel meaningful. To take care of the terminally ill, to afford them dignity in death, to know they are loved and cared for—all of this takes a lot of heart and courage.

While most of us cannot fathom working with such grief and despair day in and day out, the men and women who voluntarily choose to work in this profession find a level of fulfillment and gratification in what they do.

I've found this subject fascinating and have engaged in some compulsive reading of how people rationalize the seemingly depressive choice to work in a hospice setting. There is a startling observation that hospice care workers make: watching the process of dying makes them appreciate the value of living.

That sums it up. Nothing is more certain in life than the call of the grim reaper. But until that call comes, we need to appreciate what we have on this earth. And make our lives meaningful.

Hospice care workers understand that and remind their dying patients of a life well-lived.

In comparison, my Giving Project is a pale, insignificant step. But a step in the right direction, nevertheless.

> *Death is not the greatest loss in life. The greatest loss is what dies inside us while we live.*
>
> —Norman Cousins

AFTERWORD

 Gratitude is not only the greatest of all virtues but the parent of all others.

—*Cicero*

What started as a half-baked, random idea on my meditation cushion metamorphosized into a project that filled my life with purpose and, I dare say, a sense of adventure for twenty-one days.

As much as the Giving Project was an attempt at gratitude, it was also, undeniably, a selfish one, aimed at getting me out of my comfort zone. I learned valuable lessons on both fronts.

A common suggestion to help people get out of their comfort zones is through the "Ask Challenge." This exercise involves asking for random things from strangers, such as a discount on one's coffee at the coffee shop or asking someone to hold your place in line. I figured I'd flip it a bit and try to *give* instead of *ask*.

It wasn't any easier. I learned a lot about myself through this process.

> I had no idea I was shy. I'm not someone that gets labeled an introvert, usually. The talking to and thanking random people was awkward.
>
> Reflecting and writing about each giving experience was cathartic, no doubt, but sometimes equally cringe-inducing.
>
> I have a lot of respect for philanthropists now. I didn't particularly enjoy picking recipients out. "Playing God" may be okay for some, but not me.
>
> I think I turned overthinking into an art form.
>
> But, the most important lesson I learned is this: we find the strength to handle pain and discomfort when the goal is to benefit someone other than ourselves.

I was reminded of how meaningful it can be to cultivate the practice of gratitude. Even as someone who keeps a gratitude journal regularly, I found that the more we focus on being a helping hand to others, the more fulfilling our lives become.

Here are some more lessons I learned through the process of giving:

It's okay to give what you can even if you think it may fall short.

There are endless opportunities for giving all around us. We simply need to look.

Being human is all about being empathetic. Gratitude builds empathy.

Most people don't appreciate handouts; it's better when the giving is done as an appreciation for work performed rather than merely as a charity.

Being grateful sets off a chain of other positive habits.

FINALLY

You probably have heard of the "**Butterfly Effect**"—a concept popularized by American mathematician and meteorologist Edward Lorenz as part of the Chaos theory. Here's a simple explanation of the idea: By flapping its wings in one part of the globe, a butterfly can cause significant climatic changes (such as tornadoes) in another part of the world.

The *Butterfly Effect* is a great metaphor to model our lives on.

Through tiny, almost imperceptible acts of positive behavior, we have the capacity to cause significant, constructive changes in the world. We need to get started.

I tried to live by this motto: Give more than you take. Create more than you consume.

That, in a nutshell, is what the Giving Project is all about. The feel-good aspect of it is just icing on the cake.

AFTERWORD

After this experiment, I'm spurred on to do more. I hope you are, too.

 Just as ripples spread out when a single pebble is dropped into water, the actions of individuals can have far-reaching effects.

—Dalai Lama

NOTES

2. DAY 2: MUSIC

1. *Irrelevant trivia:* I was recently surprised to learn that the Veena is India's national instrument. I was even more surprised to know that there's such a thing as a "national instrument." One Google search led to another. I learned that "World Yarn Bombing Day" (June 11) and "Mouthguard Day" (first Monday in September) are also national calendar days. I'm now learning how to stop being surprised. At anything.

17. DAY 18:CLASH OF CULTURES

1. Completing homework on time was often thought of as the ticket for someone to go from anonymity to rocket scientist. So, well-meaning adults often asked that question—if homework was done—of the children in their lives. In other words, you could tell who the caring elders in your life were based on who asked you about your homework.

ACKNOWLEDGMENTS

Firstly, a thank you to my editor, Jessica Riordan, for taking my raw and often discombobulated words, and turning them into a coherent story.

My sincere gratitude to my dearest local friends for your unwavering encouragement and support of my blogging and writing journey. Special thanks to Divjyot for being my sounding board and guiding me through this process.

I'm very grateful to my extended family, especially my cousins Chitra and Priya, for always reading everything I publish on my blog and for your help, advice, and reassurance, and to my sister, Anupama, for believing I could actually write a book.

I can't say enough to thank all my friends and other readers of my blog in various parts of the world: your continued support of my somewhat long and rambling articles means a lot.

Of course, I'm nothing without my family—mom, my dear husband, and darling daughter. I owe a lot to them and for their support, especially for treating me like a valued houseguest and letting me hide upstairs (working, of course) most of this year .

Most importantly, to the people featured in the essays and countless others who make our lives better every day: any appreciation of your work is bound to fall short. Thank you!

Miss you, dad.

ABOUT THE AUTHOR

Aruna Gobalan (pronounced Go-bah-lun) is the creator of the self-improvement blog *Partably*. She loves personal growth projects and hopes to inspire others undertake self-improvement journeys. She is well-traveled and lives in California with her husband, daughter and mom. This is Aruna's first book.

Website: www.partably.com

Facebook: /partably

www.ingramcontent.com/pod-product-compliance
Lightning Source LLC
Chambersburg PA
CBHW020912080526
44589CB00011B/566